DESIGN AND MAKE

DECORATIVE DETAILS

HEATHER LUKE

NEW HOLLAND

For Lisa

———————

First published in 1997 by
New Holland (Publishers) Ltd
London • Cape Town • Sydney • Singapore

24 Nutford Place
London W1H 6DQ
United Kingdom

80 McKenzie Street
Cape Town 8001
South Africa

3/2 Aquatic Drive
Frenchs Forest, NSW 2086
Australia

ISBN 1 85368 942 4 (hbk)
ISBN 1 85368 943 2 (pbk)

Managing Editor: Coral Walker
Photographer: John Freeman
Designed by: Grahame Dudley Associates
Illustrator: Claire Davies

Reproduction by cmyk, South Africa
Printed and bound in Spain by Book Print, S. L.

ACKNOWLEDGEMENTS
Thanks to all those without whom this book, and indeed, this series, would not have been
possible. To John for his skill with juggling light and f-stops. For the dedication of the team
at New Holland, the designers and last, but not least, my soft furnishings team.
Special thanks and appreciation to Sarah Taylor, Mary Stewart-Wilson, Andrew and Annie
Stewart, Jano and Johnie Clarke, Carol Hicks, Dibby Nethercott and Elizabeth Peck for
allowing us to photograph and so share their beautiful homes.

For soft furnishings course details contact Calluna Workshops, Hill House, Creech St
Michael, Taunton, Somerset TA3 5DP. Fax: 01823 443335.

CONTENTS

INTRODUCTION

Throws have become one of the most useful accessories in recent years, dressing up a dull dining room chair, or brightening a dreary sofa.

According to Mies van der Rohe, the 20th-century architect renowned for his dramatic, uncluttered buildings: 'God is in the details'. Whether describing the shafts of sunlight highlighting the woven design of a damask tablecloth, or citing the perfect position for a painting, the finishing touches, decorative details and accessories, are indeed the soul of any home. These special touches reflect individual personalities and interests in ways which the architecture of a building and the choice of larger, more permanent furnishings cannot.

For most of us, the choice of house style, furniture and decorating colours is a series of compromises, compounding location, budget and the preferences of those living together. Details are small but immensely significant, and might be temporary or long lasting – a single lily or a collected group of pictures are both decorative details, both demanding their own space and attention, but with a rather different time scale and economic consideration. It is in the choosing and placing of decorative details that a house evolves, slowly but surely, into a home. Show homes can be furnished in one long shopping day, but real homes need the attention and character development which only time can supply.

Ever since lacquered furniture, ceramic vases, tea caddies and chintz cloths were brought back from the Far East, travel has played an extremely important part in the decoration of a home. Holiday purchases of batik, bejewelled Indian cottons and silks, brightly coloured South American textiles, rough woven cottons from Greek islands, antique country quilts – all can be draped or stitched to make perfect accessories and furnishings throughout the house.

Decorative details can be used to accentuate a particular colour, shape or style in a room, provide a focal point, or blend with the other furnishings. A costly fabric, well out of reach for a larger project, can be justified for a single item.

Individual taste can be accommodated in the details – a passion for paisley can be indulged in sofa throws, a favourite printed fabric far too demanding for a larger area might find a place draped over a table, pinned or upholstered to a screen. Irresistible fabric remnants discovered on market stalls, or in antique shops and fabric sales, can find their place as picnic basket linings, laundry bags, shoe box covers or napkins.

If you can't decide whether to make tablecloths in plaids or floral prints, use both. Layer cloths and mix napkins, ringing the changes for different times of day or seasons of the year.

Decorating and updating your home – although tremendous fun –

is a lifetime's project. The secret is not to take decorative accessories too seriously – even the most experienced interior decorators do not always get it right. Success is often the result of many hours of decision and anguish as ideas are tried and rejected, mistakes made and risks taken, but when a room works, the pleasure is long-lasting and the trouble taken well worthwhile.

BASIC TECHNIQUES

STITCHES

Hemming stitch

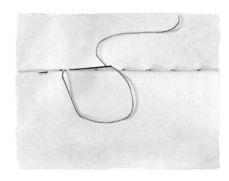

Used for hemming unlined covers, each stitch should be roughly 1.5 cm (⅝ in) in length. Slide the needle through the folded hem, pick up two threads of the main fabric, and push the needle directly back into the fold.

Ladder stitch

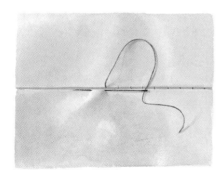

Ladder stitch is used to join two folded edges invisibly together. Slide the needle along the fold 5 mm (¼ in) and straight into the fold opposite. Slide along for 5 mm (¼ in) and back into the first fold, again directly opposite.

Herringbone stitch

Herringbone is used over a raw edge which is covered by another fabric. It is worked in the opposite direction to all other stitches.

Each stitch should be about 3 cm (1¼ in). Stitch into the hem from right to left. Approximately 1.5 cm (⅝ in) to the right make a stitch into the fabric picking up two threads. Pull through and stitch 1.5 cm (⅝ in) to the right making a stitch into the hem.

Slip stitch

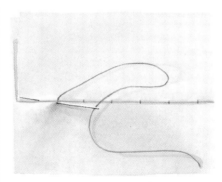

This is used for stitching linings. Make each stitch approximately 1.5 cm (⅝ in). Slide the needle through the fold by 1.5 cm (⅝ in) and pick up two threads of the opposite fabric. Push the needle back into the main fabric exactly opposite and slide through a further 1.5 cm (⅝ in).

Buttonhole stitch

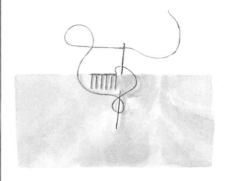

Used of course for buttonholes, but also wherever a raw edge needs to be strengthened or neatened. Work from left to right with the raw edge uppermost. Push the needle from the back to the front, approximately 3 mm (⅛ in) below the edge. Twist the thread around the needle and pull the needle through, carefully tightening the thread so that it knots right on the edge of the fabric to form a ridge.

Blanket stitch

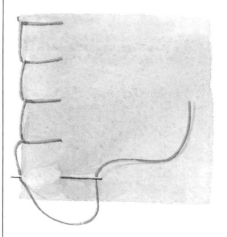

Originally used to neaten the raw edges of woollen blankets, its use is now mainly decorative. It is most comfortable worked from the side with the edge towards you. Push the needle from the front to the back, about 6 mm (¼ in) from the edge (this measurement will vary with large or small items). Hold the thread from the last stitch under the needle and pull up to make a loop on the edge.

Lampshade stitch

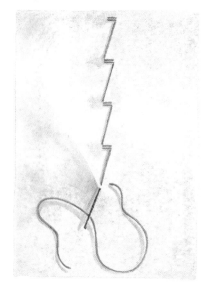

This is the most effective stitch for sewing lampshades and linings to their frame. Make a double vertical stitch about 3 mm (⅛ in) deep, bringing the thread out at the top. Take the thread down diagonally roughly 1 cm (⅜ in) and make another vertical double stitch. Repeat, adjusting the stitch to suit the frame and any pleats which you need to catch in place.

PINNING

When pinning two layers of fabric together or piping on to fabric,

always use horizontal and vertical pins to keep the fabric in place from both directions. The horizontal pins need to be removed just before the machine foot reaches them and the vertical ones – or cross pins – can remain in place, so the fabrics are held together the whole time.

SEAMS

Flat seam

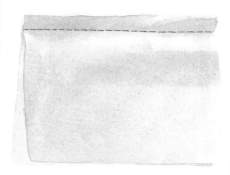

The most common and straightforward seam for normal use. With right sides together, pin 1.5–2 cm (⅝–¾ in) in from the edges at 10 cm (4 in) intervals. Pin cross pins halfway between each seam pin. These cross pins will remain in place while you are stitching to prevent the fabrics slipping. Once machine-stitched, open the seam flat and press from the back. Press from the front. Now press from the back, under each flap, to remove the pressed ridge line.

French seam

Use this seam for fine fabrics. Pin the fabrics together with the wrong sides facing. Stitch 5 mm (¼ in) from the raw edges. Trim and flip the fabric over, bringing the right sides together. Pin again, 1 cm (⅜ in) from the stitched edge and stitch along this line to enclose the raw edges. Press from the right side, always pressing the seam in one direction only.

Flat fell seam

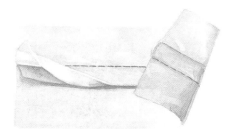

Use for heavier weight fabrics. Pin the fabrics together with the right sides facing and stitch 1.5–3 cm (⅝–1¼ in) from the raw edges. Trim one seam to just under half. Fold the other over to enclose the raw edge. Press down. Stitch close to the fold line.

MITRED CORNERS

For a neat and professional finish, you may need to mitre the hemmed corners.

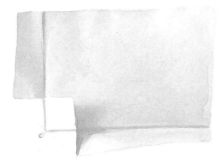

1. Press the side seam over and the hem up. Position a pin through the point of the corner.

2. Open out the folds and turn in the corner at a 45° angle, with the pin at the centre of the fold line.

3. Fold the hem up and the sides in again along the original fold lines. Keep the pin on the point and make sure the fabric is firmly tucked into the folded lines.

MAKING TIES

Ties are useful and decorative and used extensively for soft furnishings and accessories around the home.

Folded ties

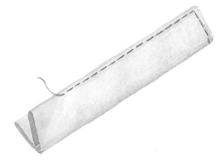

Cut a strip of fabric four times the width of your finished tie and 3 cm (1¼ in) longer.

Press one short end under by 1 cm (⅜ in). Press in half lengthwise, fold each side to the middle, press, fold and stitch close to the folded edges.

Rouleau ties

Cut a strip of fabric four times the width of your finished tie and 3 cm (1¼ in) longer. Fold in half lengthwise, right sides together, enclosing a piece of cord which is longer than the strip of fabric. Stitch along the short side to secure the cord firmly. If the rouleau is quite wide, knot the cord as well. Stitch along the length, 2 mm (⅛ in) towards the raw edge from the centre.

Trim the fabric across the corner, pull the cord through, at the same time turning the fabric right side out. Cut off the cord at the end. Press the raw edge under and slip stitch with small stitches.

PIPING

If piping is to be used in straight lines then it will be easier to cut it straight. If it is to be bent around corners, then it should be cut on the cross. For 4 mm (⅛ in) piping cord cut 4 cm (1½ in) wide strips. All joins should be made on the cross to minimise bulk when the fabric is folded.

To cut on the straight
Cut lengths as long as possible. Hold two strips, butting the ends together as if making a continuous length. Trim away both corners at a 45° angle. Hold together and flip the top one over. Stitch where the two pieces cross.

To cut on the cross

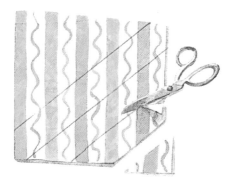

With the fabric flat on the table, fold one bottom corner as if making a 30 cm (12 in) square. Cut along the fold line. Mark pencil lines from this cut edge at 4 cm (1½ in) intervals, and cut along these lines. Hold two pieces butting the ends together as if making a continuous strip. Flip the top one over and stitch together where the two fabrics cross.

Making up and pinning on

Press seams flat and cut away excess corners. Fold in half along the length and insert the piping cord. Machine stitch to encase, approximately 2 mm (⅛ in) from the cord. Keep the fabric folded exactly in half.

Always pin piping so that the raw edges of the piping line up with those of the main fabric.

To bend piping around curves, snip into the stitching line for the piping to lie flat. For a right angle, stop pinning 1.5 cm (⅝ in) from the corner, snip the piping right to the stitching line, fold the piping to 90⁰ and start pinning 1.5 cm (⅝ in) on the adjacent side.

Joining

To join piping, overlap by approximately 6 cm (2¼ in). Unpick the casing on one side and cut away the cord so that the two ends butt up. Fold the piping fabric across at a 45⁰ angle and cut along this fold. Fold under 1 cm (⅜ in) and then pin before stitching.

BINDING

Binding one edge

1. Cut the binding strips to the width required. Join the strips to make the required length.
2. Pin the binding to the fabric, right sides together and stitch 1.4 cm (slightly less than ⅝ in) from the raw edges.

3. Neaten the raw edges to 1.4 cm (slightly less than ⅝ in). Press from the front, pressing the binding away from the main fabric. Fold the binding to the back, measuring the edge to 1.5 cm (⅝ in), keeping the fabric tucked firmly into the fold and then pin at 8 cm (3¼ in) intervals. Turn to the back of the fabric and herringbone the edge of the binding to the main fabric.

Binding a corner

Stop pinning short of the corner by the width of the finished binding. Fold binding back on itself to make a sharp angle and pin across this fold line. Pin on the adjacent side, the same distance from the edge. Stitch binding on, stopping at the pin, and secure. Begin stitching again at the same point on the adjacent side. Press to mitre. Fold fabric to the back, mitring in the opposite direction.

GLUING FABRIC TO CARD

Not all decorative accessories require sewing. Many of the storage boxes and picture frames need to be glued. However, to ensure successful results, always use a PVA glue which is water soluble and which dries clear. The best glue to use will give immediate contact, so do prepare well as mistakes cannot be rectified. Practise first with scraps if you are not confident.

Always spread glue on to the card in a thin, even layer. Place the fabic on to the table and press to remove all creases. Place the card on to the fabric, matching up any straight lines or checks along the card sides. Turn over immediately and smooth out any bubbles, checking that fabric has not shifted and the pattern is still matched correctly.

However careful you are, there will be the odd stray spots of glue, so keep a slightly damp cloth by your side to wipe away any excess immediately. If you have put too much glue on to the card and it does seep through the fabric, keep wiping the excess away with a damp cloth. Providing you are prompt, the fabric should dry without marking.

At each stage, leave the fabric covered card to dry completely. A pile of books or heavy weight on top will prevent the card bowing if the fabric is inclined to shrink.

The easiest fabrics to work with are tightly woven, mediumweight, pre-shrunk cottons, but the linens, wools and heavier cottons can be used once you have mastered the basic techniques.

PREPARATION

This is the key to successful sewing. Prepare well, and the work should go smoothly, with few errors. Look at various factors before you begin: where you are going to work, what you plan to use, linings and interlinings, card, glue and space to store your materials and equipment.

Here are some guidelines to bear in mind before you begin stitching or gluing.

THE WORKTABLE

If possible, you should stake your claim on one room which can be put aside for your own use, even if it is only while you are making your items.

A dining room or guest bedroom can be made into a temporary workroom with little effort. A worktable which is at least 2.5 x 1.2 m (8 x 4 ft) and preferably 3 x 1.5 m (10 x 5 ft) will make the whole job so much easier. You can buy a sheet of board in either of these sizes. Cover your dining table with thick felt so that the board can be rested safely on top.

Alternatively, make some sturdy legs which can be bracketed on to the underside of the board. This quickly made table can then be fitted temporarily over a guest bed. The space below can be used to store all your fabrics, and the top will be wide enough for you to work on a whole width of fabric at a time. Pure luxury compared to hands and knees on

the floor! The height of the worktable should be whatever is comfortable for you; I use a table that is 95 cm (38 in) high.

Cover the top with heavy interlining and then a layer of lining. Staple these to the underside; pulling the fabrics very taut as you go. You will now have a soft surface which is ideal for pinning and pressing.

CHECKING THE FABRIC

Before you begin to cut any fabric, check it thoroughly for flaws or incorporate them into parts that will not be seen, such as hems. If the fabric is badly flawed, return it.

Measure out each length and mark with pins to make sure that you have the correct amount of fabric. Always double check your measurements before cutting.

Fabric should ideally be cut along the grain and to pattern, but sometimes the printing method allows the pattern to move off grain. If necessary, allow the pattern to run out slightly to either side – but a 2 cm (¾ in) run-off is the most you should tolerate.

PATTERN MATCHING

It is well worth spending a little time to make sure that all fabric patterns are matched correctly at the seam on each width.

1. Place one of the lengths of fabric right side up on the worktable with the selvedge facing you. Place the next length over the first, right side down. Fold over the selvedge to reveal roughly 5 mm (¼ in) of pattern and press lightly.

2. Match the pattern to the piece underneath, and pin through the fold line along the whole length. You may need to ease one of the sides at times – using more pins will help. Go back and place cross pins between each pin. Machine or hand stitch along the fold line, removing the straight pins and stitching over the cross pins.

3. Press the seam from the wrong

side and then again from the front. Use a hot iron and press quickly. Turn the fabric over again to the back and press under the seam to remove the pressed ridges. If the background fabric is dark or you are using a woven fabric, snip into the selvedges at 5 cm (2 in) intervals. If the background fabric is light, trim the selvedges back to 1.5 cm (⅝ in), removing any printed writing.

PREPARING LININGS

Cut out your lining fabric as closely to the grain as possible. Because this is often hard to see, allow about 5 cm (2 in) extra for each cut length.

Join lining widths with flat seams. Press all seams to lay open.

To make up the hems, place one lining on to the worktable, wrong side facing up, with one selvedge exactly along the edge of the table. It is unlikely that the cut line will be exactly straight, so turn up approximately 12 cm (4½ in) along the lower edge and press in place. Keep this folded line parallel to the bottom of the table. Trim the hem to 10 cm (4 in) from the fold and then fold it in half to make a 5 cm (2 in) double hem. Pin and machine stitch close to the fold line or slip stitch by hand.

INTERLININGS

It is important that interlining is cut out following the grain. If it is not stitched exactly square, especially in any draping cloth,

after a period of time it will fall down into the hemline.

Join all widths with flat seams and trim them back to 2 cm (¾ in), snipping into the selvedge at 5 cm (2 in) intervals.

PIPING

Piping cord is available commercially in a wide range of thicknesses, graded numerically according to the diameter of the cord, corresponding roughly to the metric measurement of the diameter. Therefore a 5 mm (¼ in) diameter cord is designated No. 5. No. 00 is the narrowest cord and No. 7 is the widest one that is normally available.

Piping strips should be cut to make a 2 cm (¾ in) seam after the fabric has been folded around the cord. 5 cm (2 in) strips will fit No. 4 cord, which is the most generally used size.

Tiny pipings are used for decorative work and in places where piping is desirable but a thick edge of colour is not. Chunky piping cords are used where a statement is needed and can be very effective if self piping, so that the size rather than a contrast colour makes the detail.

COVERING CARD AND BOXES

The fabric for each section needs to be cut out beforehand with considerable accuracy, to plan how pattern repeats, checks, stripes and stylised designs can be best incorporated.

Once you have made the card patterns, or a template of the box you wish to cover, place the pieces on to the front of the fabric and mark with tailor's chalk or invisible marking pen.

Allow 2 cm (¾ in) all around each piece unless stated otherwise. These turning allowances will need to be exact because you will be relying on them to line up the edges of the card. The card will be glued to the back of the fabric which is placed face down on the table, so you might not be able to see any line or print at the time of adhesion. Once the fabric is glued to the card, it will be almost impossible to remove it.

So cut accurately and press thoroughly to remove even the smallest crease.

CUTTING CARD OR MAT

If you have self healing board all well and good, if not, it is probably not worth buying one, so use a piece of glass or board instead. Your knife will blunt a little more quickly, but blades cost considerably less than cutting boards. Either a Stanley knife or a small craft knife are suitable, but remember the blade must be very sharp. A set square and a steel ruler are essential to keep the lines and corners straight. Cut from back to front, scoring once along your pencilled line first, and then once more to cut through. A small sanding block covered with fine sandpaper can be made up and used to smooth any rough or uneven edges.

MEASURING AND ESTIMATING

TABLECLOTHS

Long cloths should be made with due consideration to the drape of the folds and whether the cloth should finish above the floor or whether it should puddle a little.

Round tablecloths

The diameter of a round cloth should be equal to the height of the table x two, plus the diameter of the table top. Hold the tape measure at the top of the table and then at an angle to estimate the length of the drape.

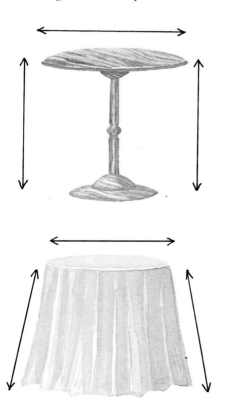

Oval tablecloths

The only way to make an accurate tablecloth for an oval table is to create a template of the top and then to add the length of the drop all around.

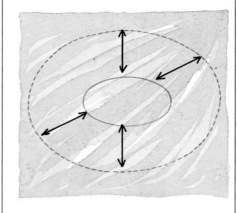

Square tablecloths

The corners of square cloths always drop below the natural bottom line of the cloth, which looks attractive if the cloth is short, but could be a hazard for a floor-length cloth. To remove the point, drape the fabric over the table and pin the folds at each corner. Draw lightly around the straight sides. Trim away the fabric and cut a straight edge in line with the marks, taking any hem allowance into consideration.

Hexagonal and octagonal tablecloths

Make a template of the table top and add the drop measurements all around. The resulting hemline will be many short, straight edges.

SEAMS

Always plan seams where they will be least obvious, for example, within a corner pleat, or along the edge of a square table. On round or oval tables try to make a seam which falls in with the draping where it will be less noticeable.

NAPKINS

Standard lunchtime napkins are approximately 40 cm (16 in) square, dinner napkins will need to be a minimum of 50 cm (20 in) square. Plan the cutting lines and try to fit three smaller napkins across the width of the fabric.

LAMPSHADES

Lampshade measurements are always given in the same order: top/slope/base.

The top and bottom measurements are all frame diameter measurements.

For gathered shades, allow for the heading and for the drop beneath the shade.

As a general rule, the diameter of the base of the frame should be equal to the height of the base. Of course, in tall candle lamps this is not the case. You will find that it is usual for candle lamps to come in two sizes. Small candle lamps are 15 x 10 x 5 cm (6 x 4 x 2 in) and larger ones 20 x 15 x 5 cm (8 x 6 x 2 in). Both of these fit the standard bulb clip fitting.

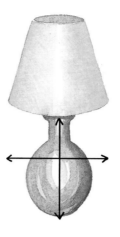

Preparing the frame

Most frames which are now available have been treated and finished with a plastic coating in white or off-white. If there are any lumps or bumps, sand them smooth. Check to see that there are no holes – if there are, dab on some enamel or household gloss paint and leave to dry. It is important that frames are completely sealed, as most cotton and silk shades can be washed gently to remove grime. However, should the frame become rusty, marks will penetrate the fabric and leave unsightly stains.

Frames can always be painted with gloss paint if you want to change the colour. For instance, if you should choose to make a dark red shade without a lining, the white frame beneath will look ugly and might show through.

Binding the frame

You will need to bind the top and bottom rings with narrow tape to provide a surface into which to pin and stitch.

Cut off a length of tape approximately three times the length to be covered. Roll it up into a ball and keep in the palm of your hand.

The last thing you want is lengths of tape flapping around.

You need to keep the tape as taut as possible, because if the binding is loose, the fabric which is stitched to the binding will be able to twist around and any pleats will distort.

1. Begin by holding the top of the shade uppermost and one strut facing you, keeping the remainder of the frame resting on your lap. Starting at the top of one strut, twist the tape around it as shown.

2. Overlap each twist by approximately one third. Keep one finger on the last twist at all times, sliding your finger around the ring as you go. Finish where you started with a figure of eight loop. Pull tight and secure with a couple of back stitches. Bind the bottom ring in the same way.

DRESSING
AND DISPLAY
TABLES

Any obsolete desk or table can be turned successfully into a dressing table – just add a larger top, make curtains to fit underneath and a cover to fit over the top

Display tables and dressing tables are important as functional pieces of furniture but can also be used to balance colour and weight within a room. Dressing tables need to be situated close to natural light and can fill some of the more awkward spaces in a room effectively – between two windows with a mirror above, in a wide bay, or an otherwise 'dead' corner area with pictures and prints hung discerningly around.

Display tables, true to their description, are tables on which to display things, whether just a simple lamp, vase of flowers, a few framed photographs or a complete personal collection, perhaps special pieces of china or glassware. The cloth, therefore, must balance the room colourings and style, be an item in its own right and still perform the duty of leading the eye to the display on top.

Fabrics need to be considered carefully for colour and texture within the room's colour scheme. Cost might be a large factor as most display cloths require at least 6 metres (7 yards) of fabric – perhaps the option of hand painting or stencilling calico or artist's canvas is an idea to be considered. Above all, the fabric must drape well. Decoration can be chosen from a huge selection of ropes, cords, cut fringes and bullions. Or, to 'ground' the cloth, simply but effectively, you might use more fabric to make a frill or ruff, to roll a quilted border, or to bind the edges in a complementary fabric.

DRESSING TABLE

As purely feminine pieces of furniture, dressing tables can be embellished or simplified, but should reflect the character of the owner. Romantic layers of lace, organdie and muslin decorated with roses and ribbons; floral prints decorated with lace-edged frills; a plain chintz undercloth with an embroidered shawl draped over or silk tulle with rows of ribbons will be bliss for one person but a complete anathema to another.

For practical purposes, the skirts are made up as curtains, to hang from a curtain track fitted beneath the tabletop. This means that they can open and close to access drawers or shelves and be removed easily for laundering.

If you are reclaiming an old table or desk, you may need to fit a new lid which extends 5-6 cm (2-2¾ in) in all directions to take the curtain track. Choose a narrow track which will bend tightly around the corners and hold the heading as straight as possible.

The lid may be upholstered with the valance stitched or tacked around, in which case a glass top should be cut to protect the fabric which cannot easily be cleaned. Alternatively, the lid and valance can be made as one, with the valance stitched to the top. To prevent the whole thing sliding around, small flaps need to be stitched inside – at each corner and halfway along each side should be adequate – and then pinned to the underside of the lid.

MAKING UP

Measure or make a template of the dressing table top. Measure the overall drop for the skirt and allow at least double fullness. Estimate the depth needed for the valance and check the proportions by pinning a strip of paper in position. Allow two or two-and-a-half times fullness for a gathered frill and three times fullness for box pleats.

Cut out the fabric pieces adding 1.5 cm (⅝ in) for all seams, 6 cm (2¼ in) for the skirt hems, 4 cm (1½ in) for the valance hem and 4 cm (1½ in) for the skirt heading. Cut out linings to match.

Fitting a dressing table into the corner provides a practical solution to an otherwise dead space. Meadow flowers on a ticking stripe line the delicate toile de jouy which gives such charming character to a country-style bedroom.

1. Pin the lining to the wrong side of the top piece. Tack together and make up as one. Make piping and pin all around. Snip as needed to accommodate corners and curves. Stitch close to the piping stitching line.

2. To make the valance, pin the fabric and lining together along the bottom long edge. Press the seam towards the lining and fold so that 2.5 cm (1 in) of main fabric shows on the back. Pin along the length and trim away excess lining. Stitch gathering threads 1.5 cm (⅝ in) from the raw edge or mark out the pleat positions allowing three times fabric for each finished pleat. If the dressing table is fitted into a recess, trim away any excess fabric at the ends and close the opening. If free standing, join the ends to make a complete circle.

3. Pin the valance to the top and stitch close to the stitching line. If the table fits into a corner and the valance does not extend to all sides, stitch small flaps to the other sides to enclose the raw edges. When the top is put back on to the dressing table, these flaps can be pinned to the underside to stop any slippage.

4. To make the skirt, join widths as necessary. Press a 6 cm (2¼ in) hem to the wrong side, press a side turning of 3 cm (1¼ in). Mitre the corners (see page 6) and herring-bone stitch all around.

5. Join lining widths as necessary. Place the lining over, wrong sides facing and lock stitch to the main fabric along the seams and halfway across each width. Score the lining around the hem and sides following the folded edge. Trim to this line. Fold the raw edges under 1.5 cm (⅝ in) at the sides and 3 cm (1¼ in) on the hem. Slip stitch neatly all around.

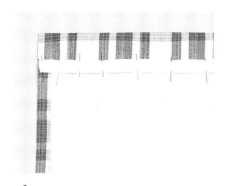

6. Measure the overall drop from the hem to the heading and fold the excess fabric over on to the lining. Pin and stitch curtain heading tape between 2 and 4 cm (¾-1¼ in) down – hook up a section and hang on to the track to test the drop and determine exactly how far down to stitch the tape.

7. Pull up the skirts and hook to the track, fit the top over the table and finger press the piping around the edge so that the valance falls straight. Pin flaps or tabs to the underside to prevent the top slipping around.

These curtains could be finished in many different ways. Try lining with a contrast colour, binding all around to pick up a colour or to contrast, or adding frills, fringes or braids to the hem to add weight and flounce.

DISPLAY TABLECLOTHS

Choosing a fabric with a small pattern in colouring similar to the sofa and to the floor rugs, allows the tables to perform a supporting role, being attractive but not dominant.

When a display table takes a central position, for instance in the centre of a hallway or large bay window, then the tablecloth fabric must be chosen for effect and will need to be beautiful in its own right. Experiment with an exotic print or richly coloured damask – sheens and rich textures are essential for full effect.

Display tables are usually round but can also be rectangular, oval or hexagonal. On an oval table, the fabric will fall almost straight along the sides, draping into folds around the curved ends.

Rectangular and square table-cloths might be fitted and boxed, but if a one-piece cloth is made and left to fall, pleats will form at each corner with the hem draping on to the floor in points.

Hexagonal and octagonal tables look interesting and should be chosen when the table is designed to take a prominent position, such as the centre of a large hall where there is walkway all around, or in the dining room with a seat placed at each side. On this style of table, the fabric will fall flat along each side and into automatic pleats at each corner. The hem will need to be cut so that the flat panels fall straight rather than draping on to the floor, and the top of each 'pleat' will need some sort of decoration – perhaps a bow, a rosette or a large button.

Whatever style is chosen, the making method remains the same. Measure carefully, and plan seams to be as unobtrusive as possible (see pages 12-13).

Left: Chunky fan-shaped edging in wool picks up all of the colour tones from this crewel worked cloth, while the cord around the hem of the undercloth actually matches nothing but echoes everything.

Right: Sofa tables serve a double purpose – here, the primary function is to provide a place for the lighting needed at either side of the sofa, but there is still room to display decorative objects and family photos. When entertaining, the lights stay in position, but the decorative items could make way for glasses and dishes of appetizers.

MAKING UP

For a circular cloth

Cut fabric pieces allowing 1.5 cm (⅝ in) for all seams and 3 cm (1¼ in) for the hem. Join widths as necessary – always keeping a full width for the centre panel with seams at either side.

1. Cut and join any lining or interlining. Fold the seamed fabric into four, making sure layers are absolutely flat. From the centre, measure and mark the tablecloth radius, including the hem allowance. Pencil a continuous line between the marks. Cut through all four layers, along this line.

2. Press the hem allowance to the wrong side, pinning to ease the fullness. Herringbone stitch all around, using stitches approximately 1.5 cm (⅝ in) in length.

3. Place the lining over, matching up the seams. Lock stitch the two fabrics together along the seams. With the end of your scissors, score the lining, following around the circumference of the cloth. Trim to this line. Fold under 1.5 cm (⅝ in) and slip stitch the lining in place.

Interlining

Interlining adds body and weight to a cloth, improving the drape considerably. A fine fabric can be made to feel heavy and a textured fabric can be given extra depth. Choose interlining which is similar in content to the main fabric. Another advantage with adding interlining is that there are no stitches visible from the front.

Cut and join widths as for the main fabric. Place on to the top fabric, wrong sides facing and lock stitch together along the seams. Trim the interlining hem so that it finishes 3 cm (1¼ in) inside the main fabric and herringbone the raw edge in place. Fold the main fabric hem over and herringbone to the interlining. Line as before in step 3.

Hems

Tablecloths hang and drape better if the hem has some weight to it. Cord, braid or fringing can provide the necessary substance. Applying a bought trimming is less time-consuming than making bound edges or frills, but tends to be more expensive.

Adding cord

Slip stitch cord to the very edge of the hem – in fact take the stitches right into the fold line. Pick up a couple of threads from the cord, keeping the stitches even. Stitches should be tight enough so that the cord does not gape, but loose enough that the fabric does not pucker.

Applying braid

Stitch braid on from both sides. Use a small running stitch in the same direction as the woven braid, matching the thread exactly.

This deeply frilled undercloth is the perfect foil for the sumptuous lace and patchwork overcloths.

TABLECLOTH

Summer fruits over a lively ochre check fabric bring an atmosphere of light-hearted sophistication to the corner of a formal dining room. The edgings for both cloths blend with the main fabric – stronger colours would have been too overpowering and detracted from the whole. Binding hems gives a neat finish and helps 'ground' the cloth.

DESIGN AND MAKE DECORATIVE DETAILS

To make a bound hem

Cut the cloth fabric without adding the hem allowance. Cut and join a bias strip from the binding fabric 6 cm (2¼ in) wide and as long as the circumference of the cloth.

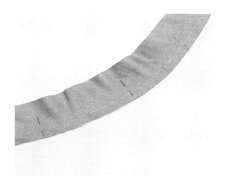

1. Pin the binding to the hem, right sides together and stitch 12 mm (½ in) from the raw edges. Use the machine foot to give you an accurate guide.

2. Press the edging fabric away from the cloth and fold under, making sure that an even 1.5 cm (⅝ in) is showing.

3. If the cloth is to be lined, herringbone stitch all around.

If interlined, add the interlining as before (see page 20) and stitch to the seam rather than to the fold in the binding.

4. Place the lining over, matching seams, and lock stitch together along the seam lines. Score the lining all around the hemline with the point of your scissors. Trim carefully along this line. Fold 1.5 cm (⅝ in) under and slip stitch to the binding. The lining fold should run along the binding seam line.

If unlined, fold the binding in twice to conceal the raw edges leaving 1.5 cm (⅝ in) showing on both sides. Slip stitch into the stitching line.

EDGINGS

Tablecloths which fall simply and straight to the ground always look so forlorn when compared to a heavily padded cloth made long enough to drape on to the floor. Binding the lower edge or adding a chunky cord will add weight to help the draped folds sit well on the floor. Corded edges can be added to lengthen a cloth which is a touch too short, or to disguise a worn or marked edge.

HEM FINISHES

A tablecloth which has no weight falls straight to the floor in limp folds. Adding interlining and lining improves the body of the fabric. Extending the length of the drop so that the folds of the cloth fall outwards and catch on the floor, also improves the drape. But more weight is needed if the cloth is to stay draped on its own. Bought trimmings, such as a heavy cord, allow the fabric to be moulded into shape, while a bullion or tasselled fringe will catch on the floor and pull the folds out. A frill performs the same function, but is too feminine for many situations; an attached roll allows the cloth to be positioned in wide scallops; an applied border adds weight discreetly.

1. A padded, quilted border adds weight and helps the cloth to hang and pleat neatly. Made from the same fabric, the border is quite discreet, the only detail being the piping at the top and bottom in a closely related colour. Vary the look by combining other colours. Try terracotta fabric bordered in black with blue/green piping. Or experiment with natural linen which would look effective with a dusty pink floral border, piped in soft pink.
2. Frilled hems are eminently suited to more feminine bedrooms and bathrooms. This deep frill catches on the floor and helps to hold the folds away from the table. Stitch the frill so that the bottom is approximately 1 cm (½ in) longer than the cloth behind it. A short frill stitched

2

3

4

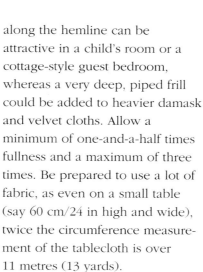

5

along the hemline can be attractive in a child's room or a cottage-style guest bedroom, whereas a very deep, piped frill could be added to heavier damask and velvet cloths. Allow a minimum of one-and-a-half times fullness and a maximum of three times. Be prepared to use a lot of fabric, as even on a small table (say 60 cm/24 in high and wide), twice the circumference measurement of the tablecloth is over 11 metres (13 yards).
3. A jumbo cord in two-tone green and cream adds weight and tradition to a lined tablecloth. It

also adds an extra colour dimension and provides a neat finishing touch.
4. Perhaps the simplest of finishes – layers of cloths in pretty provençal prints and large checks create several 'hems' or borders; the top cloth anchors the ones beneath in place.
5. A rich, crewel embroidered overcloth has been given a smart finishing touch with an attractive edging of two-colour fringing. Braid or fringing can also be used to make a too-short cloth that little bit longer and to add weight to any fabric.

STOOLS AND SIDE TABLES

Checks of any size have always been high on the list of choices for children's rooms. Spray with a water resistant finish and vacuum regularly to keep the fabric dust-free and at its best.

One of the most important rules when planning the position of your furniture is that, where possible, each seat should have its own light and its own table, and be at least large enough to place a book and a cup and saucer. I would add that a footstool at seat height would also be one of my priorities.

Tables come in all shapes and sizes, but there are other objects that can be pressed into use as small tables, including tin boxes, old chests, wooden boxes or trays on stands. The table shown here can be covered with a floor length cloth for a change of style; transformed into a stool by adding a plump cushion; or it can be topped with glass to provide an easy-to-clean surface.

The coffee tables, side tables, bedside tables, stools and luggage racks shown on the next few pages are plain wooden frames which can be made easily by anyone with basic woodworking skills. They can then be covered in almost any fabric complementary to any furnishing style. For example, the chintz patterned in grey and blue (see page 30) is perfect for a traditional stool, while a blue gingham (opposite) is a good choice for a child's room.

Leather, suede, fake crocodile or snakeskin, cotton prints, plains and checks, as well as wool plaids, tweeds and printed linens, are good to work with. The chosen fabric must be pliable but not too springy, must accept glue and not be too keen to fray, and above all, must be easy to clean. Spray with a water resistant product to repel spills and keep vacuumed to prevent particles of dirt lodging between the fibres.

DESIGN AND MAKE DECORATIVE DETAILS

LUGGAGE RACKS

It is possible to find old luggage racks at a reasonable cost which can be covered, but failing that, they are a fairly simple item for a carpenter to make. Instead of square legs you might choose round poles – the method for covering remains the same, except that poles will be screwed together rather than jointed. Choose a fabric which will withstand wear and tear.

MAKING UP

You will need PVA glue and a brush approximately 2.5 cm (1 in) wide. Cut four pieces of fabric the length of each leg plus 15 cm (6 in), and wide enough to fit easily around each leg. Cut four more pieces for the shorter horizontal bars at the top and bottom.

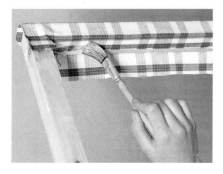

1. Cover the outside legs first. Lay one strip of fabric along the length, placed so that the overlapped edge will be on the inside of the leg, against one corner and facing downwards. Make glue spots at each end of the leg to hold the fabric in place while you are working, or lightly glue the inside piece as far as the leg joint.

2. Snip around the leg joins carefully to leave flaps approximately 1.5 cm (⅝ in) deep against the adjacent leg. Glue these in place, always using a point turner or knitting needle to push the fabric right into the joint. You will need to look at the two legs and think the process through before you cut – it is very easy to make a mistake at this point.

3. Fold the fabric right around the leg and trim away any excess on the width, keeping the edge very straight and neat. Glue and hold in place until the PVA has set so that the raw edge has no chance to fray back.

4. Repeat this procedure with the inside leg. Neaten the top and bottom of each using the spare fabric to cover the open ends.

5. Cover the lower rails. Fold the raw edges under on both sides so that the fabric exactly fits between the legs. Glue around the leg, again with the overlapped edge on the inside and facing downwards, at the same time covering all of the flaps from the previous working.

6. To cover the top rails, plan the overlap and pin the fabric along the outer edge. Fold the raw edges under at either end and cut the fabric so that it folds back to make mitred corners. Glue the corners down and then the rest of the fabric to cover the rail completely.

7. Staple wide braid to the top of one rail – the raw edge should face outwards and the spare length should drop into the middle of the rack. Wrap the braid around so that the raw edge and the staples are covered, stretch to the opposite side and wind around as tightly as possible. You will need to push the raw edge between the braid and the top of the rail. Fix as close to the top rail as possible

Luggage racks are perhaps only essential furniture in hotels, but do make pretty alternatives for the end of any bed, not to sit on but to hold either an extra blanket or the folded-back bedcover at night.

COVERING A STOOL OR SIDE TABLE

To cover the table on page 27 or the stool shown here, follow the basic gluing and neatening methods described in the steps for the luggage rack.

First cut the table/stool top allowing 1.5 cm (⅝ in) all around for seams. Cut four leg pieces, wide enough to wrap around the widest part of the leg, plus 1.5 cm (⅝ in) all around. Cut four pieces to cover each side skirt, allowing enough fabric to return to the inside top.

Stitch piping around the top piece. Attach one leg piece against the wood with the centre along the outer leg edge. (Use masking tape or drawing pins to hold the fabric securely at the top, bottom and around the leg.)

Make pencil lines on the wood, straight from the leg/table skirt join to the top of the table. Trim away the fabrics to 1.5 cm (⅝ in) beyond the pencilled lines on both sides of the leg. Snip at right angles to the leg/skirt join, but leave the 'flaps' intact. Fold under 1.5 cm (⅝ in) on each side so that the folded edges line up with the pencilled lines.

Make the other three legs the same and pin each to a corner of the table top. Pin the four skirts to the table top, just overlapping each leg piece. Stitch around close to the piping line. Cover the wooden table top with a layer of polyester wadding and fit the cover over. Staple or tack the skirts to the inside, hand stitch the leg folds to the skirts, and cover the legs using glue and staples.

Make a boxed or piped cushion to fit the top of the 'table' to make it into a comfortable stool.

For a formal room, choose a firm foam filling covered with a layer of polyester wadding. A country-style stool will need a softer, more relaxed, down and feather filled cushion.

Above: A plump feather cushion immediately transforms the crisp, tailored look of this table into a welcoming stool.

Right: Too small to risk becoming a general 'dumping ground', this elegant little table sits usefully by the front door to receive a hat, gloves or scarf.

TABLECLOTHS AND SETTINGS

Crisp white never fails to please, whether as rough cotton piqué in the kitchen or best linen or cotton damask in the dining room. Perfect in its simplicity, with only a glass of wine and a few black olives, white is equally comfortable as a background for naive country pottery and colourful napkins or dressed with the very best china and silver.

Kitchen tablecloths are altogether more relaxed and interchangeable than their more formal dining room counterparts as they are easily laundered. A good selection of similarly coloured cloths supplies the basis for interesting table decorations. Squares and rectangles are the easiest to work with as they fit round tables as well. Layering several cloths of varying fabrics also works a treat and can be immensely versatile.

Checks, stripes and florals, small stylized prints and neat provençal prints combine together successfully, mixing and matching, and providing an adaptable base for a number of occasions. Choose colours of the same tonal range for uncomplicated harmony.

Hem the sides by hand or machine or satin stitch around in a contrast colour – make two or three rows using contrasting coloured threads. Ribbon, braid or tape in plain colours make a good finish for the edges of a patterned cloth, while braids woven with decorative motifs look most effective against a plain one – press the raw edges to the front, mitre the corners and enclose inside the braid.

LAYERED TABLECLOTHS

Tablecloths are so easy to make that you can keep a selection in several sizes, colours and patterns in the cupboard, ready for impromptu entertaining. Squares and rectangles are the easiest cloths to make and they fit round tables too. Measure the top of the table, push a dining chair in place, then measure from the table edge to the seat of the chair. Add this to each side of the tabletop measurements. Usually 15-20 cm (6-8 in) is adequate for a kitchen table; add slightly more for a formal dining room. Allow 3 cm (1¼ in) all round for hem allowances. Make up in the usual way.

IDEAS FOR CORNERS

Decorating the table can be as much fun as preparing the meal and choosing the crockery. I often use plain cloths, decorating the centre with fresh, expendable greenery, from the garden – a few lenghs of green creeper placed across a white tablecloth can look effortlessly dramatic against glass or silver. I like to tie plain, white napkins with fronds of honey-suckle or wisteria and push a daisy or rose into the top.

A patterned cloth provides its own decoration. Calico or linen can make inexpensive cloths but sometimes you might like to embellish the corners.

1. Use a button to hold folds of fabric in gentle cascades. Cover the button in fabric, or choose leather, metal, an elaborate bejewelled creation, or children's motifs, such as teddies, boats or frogs for a birthday party.

2. A simple bow makes a more elaborate decoration, perhaps for a wedding or anniversary. Lengths of fabric to match or contrast, ribbons or cotton tapes – experiment with pinking the edges, or cut gingham on the cross and gently fray the sides.

3. Extravagant loops of satin, petersham or florist's ribbon and a dried hydrangea provide the decoration for an autumn supper. Replace the dried flower with fresh for a summer party. Bind the stem with damp cotton wool to preserve blooms.

1

2

3

PLACEMATS

Whatever the cloth or table surface beneath, once the table is prepared, it is the place setting which takes the attention. How much more inviting and special is a bowl of homemade soup when presented on an interesting, colourful placemat.

Try to buy quilted fabric but if you can't find anything you really like, then quilt your own before making up. To find the best size for you, lay a full table setting and practise with paper placemats until you have determined the perfect size. An interesting, complementary lining makes all the difference,.but choose one with the same washing requirements.

MAKING UP

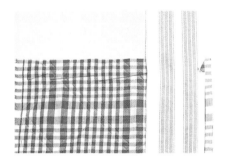

1. Cut the placemat to size, centring any pattern, stripe or check. Cut a length of contrast fabric the circumference of the placemat and 8 cm (3¼ in) wide for a 2.5 cm (1 in) finished edge. Pin the binding to the right side, setting the edge 1 cm (¾ in) from the placemat edge. Stop 2.5 cm (1 in) from the corner.

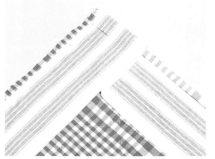

2. Fold the binding edge back at an exact 45° angle and continue to pin along the adjacent side. Repeat with the next and following corners. Join the two ends of the binding neatly.

3. Press the seam flat and stitch the binding to the mat, exactly 1.5 cm (⅝ in) from the edge. Stop at each corner and secure. Start again on the other side of the flap, inserting the needle right against the last stitch.

4. Press the binding from the right side, away from the mat. Mitre each corner (see page 8) and fold the sides under.

5. Mitre the corners on the wrong side and turn under 1.5 cm (⅝ in) to conceal the raw edges. Slip stitch along the fold, to the stitching line. Use small stitches to prevent gaping and to make the stitching line as strong as possible.

NAPKINS

Colourful napkins provide the finishing touch to kitchen supper. Choose fabrics which will wash well and require minimum ironing. Checked fabrics are readily available and contrast well with so many other patterns or plain colours.

Lunch napkins should be at least 35 cm (14 in) square. As most fabrics are 130-135 cm (52-54 in) wide, three napkins can be cut across each width of fabric. Dinner napkins should be at least 50 cm (20 in) square, so are not as economical to cut. Always allow 3 cm (1¼ in) all around and finish with a machine or extremely tiny hand stitches.

A simple hem is all that is needed for a patterned fabric and any extraneous detail can be avoided if you have chosen an eclectic mix of colours and patterns. A classic choice of blue/white with yellow/white might look good with some

contrasting stitching. Perhaps a sharp blue edge, satin-stitched around a yellow/white napkin lying on a blue and white cloth with a yellow stitched edge.

Fray the edges for a country look. Stitch a small zig zag line approximately 3 cm (1¼ in) from the edge of each napkin. Pin the napkin to a flat surface and pull the threads one at a time from one side at a time. If the edges bind together with washing, just comb them out lightly.

Napkins are so simple to make, that there is really no excuse for not running up six or eight in matching or complementary sets. If you are making a tablecloth anyway, plan to sew napkins as well. Or make several sets, tie with ribbon or cord and present as attractive gifts.

LAMPSHADES

The prettiest piece of unlined, embroidered silk allows the light within to accentuate the beautiful and intricate work.

There cannot have been a time in history when the choice of light shades, lamps and lighting for almost every room in the house was so wide and varied.

In 1756, Isaac Ware warned that the cost of illuminating a room should be considered an important factor – firstly, in the choice of fitting, and then the effect of the household budget from there on. Of course, he only had candles to worry about!

Now we have centre lights and wall lights, floor lights and standing lights, table lamps and portable candle lamps, chandeliers, candelabra, all of which might be 'shaded' with fabric, card, glass, metal, plastic, wood or raffia.

Decide whether your room needs lampshades which are accent points (in the same way that a scarlet bow might set off a black and white evening dress), or whether these 'decorative accessories' are to become part of the whole. For example, as a yellow rose popped into a vase of pink, buff and peach roses adds a subtle dimension while immediately becoming an indefinable part of the whole.

Conventional card or pleated silk shades in tones of oyster, cream, ivory and buttermilk always deserve consideration for the amount of warm, diffused, relaxed light which they give. Avoid white or pastel shades which will throw cold light, and use mid and deep blues and greens with great care. On their own, the light given is cold and uncomfortable, but they can be made acceptable with a gold, yellow ochre or pink lining.

Rich colours such as reds, terracottas and deep corals throw light with the warmth and atmosphere of candlelight, especially if subdued further with sand- or cigar-coloured linings.

INFORMAL SHADES

Gathered shades are very simple to make and take a small amount of fabric – offcuts of furnishings fabric, the smallest piece of a favourite, extravagant fabric or simple cotton lawn can be usefully regenerated. Gathered covers need a metal or card frame beneath to hold the shape, and are usually fitted over an existing card shade, either to soften the light, to add a more feminine touch to the room, or to cover up a worn shade beneath.

MAKING UP

Measure the depth and circumference of the under shade. Allow 3-6 cm (1¼-2¼ in) to fall below the bottom of the frame and for fullness estimate one-and-a-half times the circumference. Add approximately 8-12 cm (3¼-4¾ in) for a frilled heading, or double the finished frill size plus 2 cm (¾ in) for gathering. But remember, the more fullness in the shade, the less light will be able to penetrate. Cut and join the fabric as necessary to make a full circle.

Golden toile de jouy throws a warm light and full gathers soften the direct beam, concentrating light downwards for reading. The scalloped picot edge is a pretty touch.

1. Make a template for the scalloped edge. Mark a piece of card into equal sections of between 8 and 12 cm (3¼ and 4¾ in) and then make curves within each one by drawing around a household object, e.g., a glass, a saucer or a pot lid.

2. Cut out the fabric using the template. Pin the picot edging around, 1.5 cm (⅝ in) from the edge, following the shapes of the curves and especially keeping the points sharp – the definition can easily be lost at this stage. Stitch the picot edge in place.

3. Pin the top fabric to the lining, right sides facing and stitch together, following the last stitching line.

Trim the fabric to shape, snipping right into the points. Turn to the right side and press the scalloped edge neatly.

4. The top can be finished in one of two ways.

Method 1
Measure the length of the shade from the hem upwards, including the frilled heading allowance. Fold the rest to the back. Neaten both fabrics as necessary and press the raw edge under. Stitch around, close to this fold, leaving a 2 cm (¾ in) opening next to the seam. Stitch around again 1.5 cm (⅝ in) above. Thread a ribbon through this channel and tie up when the cover sits comfortably over the under shade.

The ribbon can be used as a method for gathering, as here, or it could be decorative, in which case it needs to be threaded from the front. Cut and stitch two small buttonholes into the channel at the centre front of the shade. Pull the ribbon through and tie in a generous bow.

Method 2

Measure the length of the shade from the hem upwards, including the frilled heading allowance. Trim the front fabric away along this line. Trim the lining to approximately 4 cm (1½ in) above this line. Bring the lining over to the front and press. Fold under 1.5–2 cm (⅝–¾ in) to make a binding. Slip stitch in place.

Approximately 4–6 cm (1½–2 in) down, stitch two rows through both layers of fabric to make a channel. From the front, carefully cut and stitch two buttonholes (see page 6).. Thread the ribbon through and pull up to gather the fabric, so that the cover sits comfortably over the under shade.

This shade cover really is one of the simplest to make, especially for those who like to be able to start and finish a project within a couple of hours.

Cut, and join fabric if necessary, to make one circle, with a circumference just a little larger than the frame and roughly 30 cm (12 in) longer. Hand-stitch hems along both sides – a decorative shell stitch on the lower edge and a simple slip stitched hem at the top.

Pin the fabric to the frame with 10 cm (4 in) below and the rest above. Pleat the fabric around the top ring, dividing the fullness equally between the frame struts. Stitch the hem to the back of the top ring, also gathering in the fullness evenly. Scrunch up the deep frill and stitch randomly to hold in place. Along the base of the frame, catch up the length at each strut so that the hemline falls in soft scallops.

Classic white linen looks as at home on a wood base with country flowers as it would on a metal stand in a sophisticated white and grey apartment. The rouleau tie with curled ends adds a feminine touch to the deep box pleats.

GATHERED LAMPSHADES

Traditional styles of lampshades, whether stretched, pencil pleated or box pleated, are the best for formal rooms and lamp classic bases. On the other hand, plain card shades can be used with almost any base and in almost any style of room. Sometimes, however, less formal shades are needed and something which takes little time to make yet still gives a stylish finish is always an attractive proposition.

The fabric shades shown in this gallery are all very quick to make and slip easily over existing card shades. The basic fabric shade is the same for each one; only the trimmings have been changed.

Each one is essentially a tube of fabric with a circumference larger than the lampshade base, gathered along the top edge. Soft, draped fabrics need to be at least one-and-a-half-times fullness and fall against the shade, while heavier linens and cottons sit away from the edge to give a more rounded shape and may need little or no more than one-and-a-half times fullness for a pleasing shape.

Make sure that the fabric lampshade is deep enough to cover the card shade.

1. Off-white cottons, linens and silks always look elegant no matter how simply treated. One-and-a-half times fullness of fine linen has been box pleated to fit the top rim and finished with two lengths of wide satin ribbon, tied in a loose bow and cut into deep swallowtails.

1

2

2. Gold and white ribbon in two different widths are stitched to the lower and top edges of the shade, holding the gathers in place, with a further piece stitched inside to enclose the raw edge completely. Wired edges on both sides of the ribbon encourage the lower edge into a pretty, softly undulating form which stands away from the card shade.

3. The same linen shade adorned with rows of silk ribbon roses can be fun for a dressing table or a decorative corner in a formal room. Approximately 1 m (1 yd) of wired ribbon is needed for each large rose and 50 cm (20 in) for buds. Roll up in one hand and stitch through each layer to hold the base tightly. The wired edge allows you to re-arrange the petals however you wish.

4. Any interesting ribbon, braid or edging can be stitched to a lampshade base; in this case a calico ribbon printed with musical notes seems perfect for a bedside lamp. Natural calico forms the main body of the shade with a black flat cotton to edge both top and bottom.

It is especially important when choosing fabric for lampshades that you select the correct drape and weight for the job. Hold the fabric over the frame to see how much light will pass through and check to see whether the fabric creases badly.

Very soft, floaty silks or fine linens, for example, will just filter the light to give a soft and diffused glow, while a heavier chintz or calico will obscure the light, throwing it downwards to create pools on the surface below.

3

4

PLEATED SHADES

Pleated shades are at once elegant and informal. Silks, cotton lawns, light- to mediumweight printed cottons are all suitable fabrics – choose pale backgrounds for maximum light and warm base colours for a subdued ambience. For a moody effect, pleat heavy, glazed cottons in deep burgundy, forest greens and luxuriant terracottas – deeply pleated, these dark colours can look like rich, supple suede as the light reflects the slightly shiny and matt qualities. With all dark-coloured shades, the indirect light is absorbed, concentrating in pools above and beneath the shade.

Choose a printed pattern which will not be spoilt when gathered into tight pleats. Light background fabrics allow plenty of indirect light through while still directing most on to the table below.

MAKING UP

Prepare the shade by binding the top and bottom rings as shown on page 13.

Either the top or the bottom ring will have the fabric pleated to it, with small gathers stitched on to the opposite ring. If the shade is empire or drum in shape, (i.e. the diameter of the top and bottom rings are not too far apart) you may choose to pleat around either the top or the bottom ring.

Where there is a large difference – say with a coolie shade which has dimensions of 10 cm (4 in) at the top and 35cm (14 in) at the base – the fabric will be pleated and overlapped around the top and will be only slightly gathered around the base. If the base was given three times fullness it would be impossible to pleat the fabric around the small top ring. So, for a coolie frame, cut and join enough fabric to cover the bottom ring one-and-a-half to two times. For an empire frame, allow three times the top or bottom ring circumference. Cut each strip 4 cm (1½ in) longer than the shade depth, measuring along the slope.

1. To line the shade, estimate the amount of lining fabric needed by placing the frame on its side and marking the top and bottom of one of the struts. Roll the shade through 360°, running a pencil line around the lower edge as you go. Over-cut this piece by 6 cm (2¼ in) in all directions.

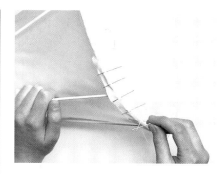

2. Drape the fabric around the outside of the shade, pinning along the seam and attaching it into the top and bottom rings. Pin and re-pin until the fabric is taut and all the wrinkles have been removed.

3. Trim to within 2 cm (¾ in) of the frame. Remove and stitch the seam from the wrong side, using a very narrow zig-zag stitch. The lining may be attached to the frame either now, or after the pleated top cover has been stitched to the frame. Pin back on to the frame – this time from the inside, again re-pinning until the lining is taut.

4. Stitch all around with lampshade stitch. Stitch at the front of the rings. Trim the lining close to the stitching line.

5. Place one width of the fabric on to the worktable and pleat up one long side, taking 3 cm (1¼ in) for each 1 cm (¾ in) of pleat. Pin to the top of the frame, keeping the pleats straight and even. Do not make machined joins – just overlap the next piece, incorporating the selvedges into the next pleat. Stitch each pleat in place, catching down each fold.

6. Attach the fabric to the bottom ring, keeping the pleats straight and evenly spaced between the frame struts. Gather evenly and pin at very close intervals so that each gather looks like a tiny pleat. Stitch in place. Trim away any excess.

7. Make small rolls of lining fabric to loop around the two frame joints on the top ring, so hiding the raw lining edge. Stitch to the frame and trim excess.

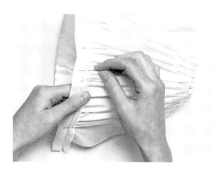

8. To bind the edge, cut a strip of fabric 4 cm (1½ in) wide, the length of the ring circumference. Press into three. Open out and pin around the ring so that 1 cm (⅜ in) is above and the rest below.

9. Stitch in place with lampshade stitch. Join the two ends on the diagonal. Fold the binding back on itself to cover all raw edges.

EDGINGS

Binding the top and bottom of the shade leaves an understated, neat finish, but you might want to add a more decorative finish – short ruffs and deep frills might suit a feminine bedroom or extend a less formal touch to a drawing room. Passementerie: braids, fringes and trimmings, offer unlimited scope for decoration. For example, a fan edging might be stitched over a deep frill, or a cord can be placed to finish the top of a plain cut fringe. Choosing colours of the same tone keeps the whole in harmony, but don't be afraid to choose bold mixes – lime green with citrus lemon or deep red with navy blue, as accessories should be used to challenge and revitalise a tired scheme.

1. Butterfly frills, made at least double fullness, are stitched on so that the top sits forwards and the rest falls straight down, concentrating the light towards the tabletop beneath.

Flat gimp, a two-coloured fan edge, a short cut fringe or twisted cord stitched over the gathering line, bring another colour and dimension to the overall shape.
2. Two-toned fan edging brings another colour into the picture. Keeping one colour to match the shade gives continuity – the other could have just as easily been a soft pink, green, coral or blue. Look for braids where the top is as interesting as the bottom.
3. Linen and silk make lovely textural and tonal combinations, especially in a neutral scheme. Deep fringing encourages the

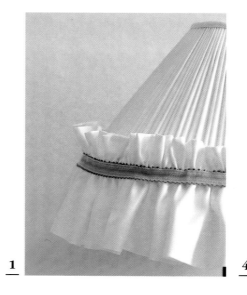

available light and the eye downwards. Some fringes have decorative tops which are beautiful in their own right; this plain edge on the other hand is quite simple.
4. This shade demonstrates a different use for the same fan edging; the lovely top on this particular one improves the look of the cut fringe dramatically.
5. A short fringe will stay tidier for a more formal room. Black threads running through give a degree of smartness.

BOX PLEATS

Box pleating produces a more formal finish than knife pleating or pleating and gathering, although the shades may be used in almost all the same situations. The making method is very similar and the same fabrics can be used. At the pleating stage, the top should be pleated up using three times fullness for each pleat, with the pleats butting up exactly. Once the top has been pinned on, each pleat should be splayed to fit the bottom ring. Red silk subdues light in such a way that the atmosphere resembles that from a candle.

PLEATED CARD SHADES

Pleated card shades are, to the relief of some, absolutely no-sew shades. Taking little fabric and time, one large or two small shades can realistically be accomplished in one evening.

You will need the top ring only for smaller shades and a frame with top and bottom rings for anything over 30 cm (12 in) across the bottom. Make sure that the fitting you buy will suit the purpose – if you have a shade carrier a single ring is enough, for a ceiling light you will need the complete gimbal fitting.

I prefer the look of fabric on pleated shades but wallpapers and decorative papers could be substituted. If you can't find the adhesive backing used here, make your own by pasting a medium weight card to the back of your fabric or paper.

MAKING UP

Measure the metal frame or an existing shade to decide the depth needed. For the depth, the fabric should extend approximately 5 cm (2 in) below the frame. For the length, you will need two to three times the finished circumference depending how small and full you want the pleats to be. It is best to test the effect of some different sized pleats with a piece of stiff paper before you start.

You will need a right angle and a metal straight edge to complete this lampshade.

Concertina pleats make an interesting variation on the rigid lines of formal checks.

DESIGN AND MAKE DECORATIVE DETAILS

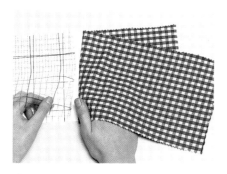

1. Cut your length of fabric and finish with pinking sheers if you have them. If not, cut the edges as cleanly as possible and avoid handling the fabric. If you have chosen a fabric which frays greatly, press the fabric on to the finest fusible interfacing you can find before you cut it. Cut the backing material to the exact size. Place the fabric over, so that as the adhesive side is unrolled you can press the fabric down with the palm of your hand, smoothing out any creases and air bubbles.

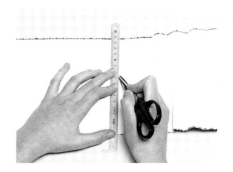

2. Trim away any excess fabric. With the aid of a metal straight edge, mark out each pleat. Use a right angle frequently to make sure that the pleats do not start to lean. Pleat up in concertina style.

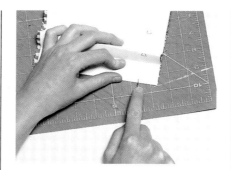

3. You will need to make a hole for the ring to pass through and it is possible to use a paper punch. However to obtain the best fit, inverted V shapes need to be cut at the inner edge of each pleat. Again test on a spare piece of paper to determine the best size, but you should just be able to press the ring in and the paper cut should close over it.

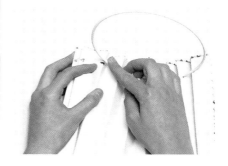

4. Press the ring into each cut and concertina the pleats together tightly. Join the ends with PVA adhesive and hold together until set. Clamp large paper clips to the top and bottom to hold the shade securely overnight.

5. Thread ribbon through at the front and tie into a bow. If the ring does show through between the pleats, you can either paint the frame to match or tone with the fabric, or wind ribbon around the ring between each pleat.

Small, candle-sized shades are a treat to make, being easy to handle and immediately rewarding. The brass ring at the top adds an attractive dimension; here it is fitted to a candle holder but it can also serve as a bulb clip for an electric light.

THROWS

Silk paisley is enchanting when scrunched over crunchy woollen country tweed, emphasising the depths of texture and colour.

Throws have become perhaps the most useful, successful and even necessary home accessory in recent years, inspired by the increasingly beautiful textures, colours and fabrics available. Couture designers have given us large shawls and wraps in luxury fabrics and stunning designs, and as Ralph Lauren, Calvin Klein, Caroline Charles and Versace have paved the way for others to turn their attention to the home market, we can expect many more lovely throws and accessories.

Any square of fabric might become a throw: if the back is as attractive as the front, all the better. Bedcovers and hangings in lovely soft natural dyes from India, lengths of exotically coloured weaves from South America, richly coloured chenilles from Italy, rustic weaves and hand embroidered linens from Mediterranean islands, can be bought from boutiques worldwide or collected on holidays. Blanket manufacturers have risen to the challenge of the continental quilt market by designing blanket throws in traditional plaids, window pane checks, tweed mixes, and linen and cotton herringbones in a variety of colours and textures.

A sublime cashmere throw can be used for warmth as a bedcover one day, thrown decoratively over a chair on another and then used to snuggle into on a cool summer evening.

VERSATILE THROWS

Throws might be draped over a sofa or folded on to a bed introducing a touch of texture, colour and glamour. Or they can serve as a fashion statement, as a throw is so much easier to change than a permanent cover.

Draped and tied over single chairs and sofas, throws can be made more permanent, taking the place of a slip cover; hung around a bed to make a luxurious canopy, thrown over a pole to dress a window or fitted to draw in the same way as curtains.

Shawls, scarves or chenille squares thrown over an arm or one side of a chair or sofa, add informality, an extra colour or a further dimension. Use throws as an inexpensive way to ring the changes – add paisley to tweed, animal print to paisley, roses to stripes, white to creams, tartan to floral chintz, soft wool cashmere to crunchy linen.

If you have made an error or are disappointed with your room, think about using one or more throws to change the balance of colour or texture or even to cover a real mistake completely. Tartan or tweed blankets folded decoratively over the back of chairs serve a double purpose – adding interest and texture to the other furnishings, but also practically – to wrap around you when in front of the fire.

1. In the fashion world, leopard and other animal prints go in and out of style from season to season and make periodic appearances in

1

the home accessory market. A throw is an ideal vehicle to provide such a fashion accessory – one year on a bed, another draped over a sofa or chair, and if washable, a fun garden rug.

2. Cashmere or cashmere and wool mix fabrics are soft and pliable, draping easily. The coffee colours and the warm texture were chosen for this winter chair cover, which is removed in the summer to reveal a light calico stripe beneath.

3. Chenille or linen squares can be draped over dining chairs to change the mood for different

occasions and changing seasons. Drape the throw over the chair, with one corner dropping just over the front of the seat. Push a fold of the fabric into the seat or back join and then tie the two side corners together at the back. Coral reds and olive greens balance the rich colours of Christmas.

4. A simple bunch of artificial berries tied together with freshly dried orange slices and a stick of cinnamon looks stunning and exudes a wonderful aroma.

5. Instead of tying at the side, knot all three corners of the throw at the centre back. Decorate with

2

3

4

5

an elaborate Christmas bouquet –
silk ribbons with fir cones, newly
picked greenery, dried orange
slices and fragrant cinnamon to fill
the room with seasonal perfume.

For a summer party you might use
crisp white linen throws adorned
with fresh lilies and roses; to keep
flowers alive incorporate damp
florist's foam or a small phial of

water. Weddings or anniversaries
provide great opportunities for
themed decoration: try a bunch of
leaves sprayed with silver and tied
with white and silver ribbons.

MIRROR AND PICTURE FRAMES

An inexpensive pine, plastic or metal dressing table mirror can be bought and covered with fabric to match curtains, bedcovers or other accessories. The padded top makes a perfect, crease-free finish a little more difficult to achieve but the added softness is well worth the extra time and effort.

Covering your own frames not only saves an enormous amount of money, but also gives you an unrestricted opportunity to choose your own colours, fabric and prints. Fabric, either padded or glued straight on, can transform inexpensive, ordinary frames into lovely accessories.

A bought frame can be covered to hold a mirror, a picture or a photograph. Don't attempt anything too large to begin with, start with a frame of a simple shape and medium size and work up. Photograph frames come in many sizes and styles to practise with – and after all, can anyone ever have too many photo frames?

You will need to find a water-soluble adhesive which will set fairly quickly, so that the fabric will not mark. Test a small piece of fabric first to see that it accepts the glue but does not absorb it too easily.

Suitable fabrics should include any which can be pulled taut without the pattern distorting, lightweight enough that the glass will still fit into the space allocated, but heavy enough that the bought frame beneath does not show through. If the bought frame is dark in colour, avoid any fabric with a light background.

When choosing a pattern, it might be as well to avoid stripes, checks or any geometric print – although they can look smart, they are very tricky for a beginner to handle. All-over designs are by far and away the most forgiving.

MAKING UP

A small print like this will need to be planned before you cut the strips. Lay the fabric over the frame and decide how the sides and corners should look. It will be virtually impossible to match any pattern at all four corners. It is usually best to choose a part of the pattern that will join on a mitre without difficulty. Corners always look better darker rather than lighter, so try to avoid having mainly background in any corner.

You will need PVA glue, a suitable working surface and – if you have access to one – a staple gun will be useful.

1. Cut four strips of fabric, one each for the top and bottom across the width and two vertical strips for the two sides, keeping the grain straight. Cut each piece 5 cm (2 in) longer than the outer measurements and wide enough to cover from the back over the front and on to the back of the frame again.

2. Cut strips of polyester wadding to fit exactly over each side and glue lightly in place. Pin one vertical and one horizontal strip together at one corner and plan the mitre. Mark the inner and outer edges of the frame with a pin. Place the pieces right sides together, pin along the marked mitre and stitch between the edge pins. Pin this corner lightly to the wadding and repeat on the remaining three corners in turn.

3. From the back, paste the width of the frame and press the fabric in place, keeping the mitred corner in position and the grain straight. Paste the inner edge of the frame and press the other side of the fabric strip in place. Pull the fabric taut enough across the frame to prevent wrinkles but not so tight that the corners are pulled away. Snip into the seam allowance so that the mitre can lie flat on the front and snip away any excess.

4. Repeat with each side and corner. Staple the fabric securely to the frame and trim away any excess fabric.

5. Cut another piece of fabric, paper-backed fabric or medium weight card to fit just inside the overall frame measurements and paste in place to cover all the untidy raw edges.

It is often difficult to find an appropriate frame, especially for a feminine-style dressing table. Instead, look to cover an inexpensive, basic wooden frame to suit your room decoration and harmonize with your furnishings. Choose a part of the pattern which will mitre well for each corner. This particular pattern is spread out a little too much to expect more than two good corners, but the overall effect works very well.

DOUBLE PHOTOGRAPH FRAME

This is a brilliant way to use up those offcuts of fabric left over from curtains, blinds, cushions and bedcovers. Making your own photograph frames gives you the chance to match or complement your other furnishings and to make them to a specific size. Perfect as a present to send abroad, a photo frame slips easily into a standard envelope with a greetings card.

MAKING UP

You will need to cut four pieces of 2 mm (⅛ in) card and two pieces of thin card to the size frame you require. Cut away the centre of two of these pieces for the front of the frame so that the opening is just smaller than your photograph.

Cut two pieces of fabric for the fronts, 2 cm (¾ in) larger all around than the card.

Place the two backs on to the fabric next to each other, but with a 2 cm (¾ in) gap in between. Cut around them, leaving 2 cm (¾ in) all round. Cut two lining pieces the width of the card and 4 cm (1½ in) longer.

You will need a 12 mm (½ in) glue brush, PVA glue, and a suitable working surface.

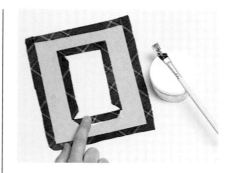

1. Paste a thin layer of glue on to the two front cards and place them centrally over the fabric. Press from the front with the palms of your hands. Cut away the centre, leaving 1 cm (⅜ in) from the card and snipping to within 2 mm (⅛ in) of each corner. Glue these flaps to the card and hold until set. Paste a brush width along the bottom of the card and glue the fabric in place. Cut away a square of fabric at each of these corners to remove the overlap. Leave to dry under a weight – a pile of books is ideal.

2. Cover the thin pieces of card with lining fabric, folding the extra length to the back. Place one lined card on to each front piece, keeping the lining side to the front and the bottom pieces together. Glue the remaining three edges of fabric over both pieces of card. Fold or mitre the top corners, snipping away any excess fabric. Leave to dry under a weight.

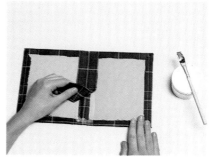

3. Glue the two back pieces to the fabric as shown. Fold the two long sides over the card and hold until set. Trim away the squares of excess fabric at the corners as before. Glue the two short sides in place, trimming the corners back to a mitre. Hold each corner until dry so that you can ensure it stays square and any frayed ends are secure. Cut a strip of fabric 4 cm (1½ in) wide and position over the gap to make a spine.

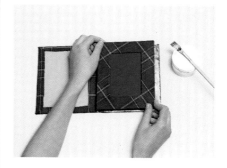

4. Paste the card sides of the frame fronts and backs. Position the fronts on to the backs, keeping the sides straight and making sure that the opening at the bottom is clear. Press again under a heavy weight – overnight or until completely dry.

Cutting a plaid to fit on the cross is most effective and avoids much time consuming matching of horizontal and vertical lines.

PICTURE BOWS

Hanging pictures is an acquired skill – learnt only by continuous trial and error and by seeing how other people have achieved attractive results.

A group of smaller pictures offers far more opportunities for varying shapes and forms than a single, larger picture. To hang a set of three, four, six or more is not difficult. First, they should be grouped in terms of content, period and size. Ideally, matching frames should be placed close together in a manner which relates to a piece of furniture beneath, or to some architectural feature, and to the available wall space.

Plan your picture arrangement on a flat surface – the floor, a bed or a large table. Copy your preferred arrangement on to a piece of brown paper or newspaper. Pin or hold against the wall to check whether the effect is as attractive in position. If the plan is accurate you can use this template to establish the final fixing positions.

Neither bows nor cords are substantial enough in their own right to hold a picture to the wall. Use traditional fixings and picture wire, making sure that the picture is really firmly hung before you play with the decoration.

Fit a decorative hook into the wall above the picture and attach your bow or cord to this with a narrow tape. Where fabric or cord needs to be attached to the back of the picture, use a piece of touch and close fastener or sticky tape and fit to the frame.

Cords

Stiff cord might be more difficult to tie, but soft cord will need stiffening with starch if the knotted form is to last. Knot and stitch into shape, immerse in liquid starch and leave to dry, or if you are unsure of the colourfastness, use starch in spray form and apply liberally.

Bows

Bows can be made from one or more lengths of ribbon in all widths and colours as long as the finished result achieves an effect complementary to both picture and setting. Strips of fabric can be tied in the traditional manner to make two loops and two tails, to make two loops and one centre tail, as a double bow to make four loops and two tails, or in three loops with one tail to resemble an Elizabethan cross.

Most elaborate sashes, swags and bows can be made from fabric which has been steeped in liquid starch. Lay on a flat surface and finger pleat into shape. Leave to dry, and you will find that the fabric has taken on your chosen shape and will retain it in a rigid and long-lasting form.

A single coloured ribbon can 'hold' a set of pictures together, picking up the colour from the wallpaper or matching with the curtains, complementing or contrasting with the colouring of the framed prints.

SCREENS

Hiding ugly pipes and to cover a window too small to be curtained, this wooden screen – slip-covered with a romantic print on one side and a striking stripe on the other – can be turned around to reveal its summer or winter colours.

Creating rooms within rooms, screens must be among the earliest form of home furnishing, as nomadic tribes sought to divide their tents with fabric panels. Later, church architects designed elaborately pierced and carved wooden and stonework partitions to screen the holy areas from the public view, and to separate the rich from the poor of the congregation.

Sometimes replacing draped rugs and tapestries, screens acted as most adaptable room dividers and efficient draught excluders in front of non-functioning fireplaces, behind a low chair, or in front of an ill-fitting door. For modesty, simple screens provided private changing areas in shared rooms and by contrast, elaborately decorated, carved, gilded or painted screens become fashionable items of furniture in a lady's boudoir.

However, whether pierced, embossed, studded, upholstered or painted, screens have for centuries been decorative as well as functional. Decoration, is most notable on antique European screens. Some were upholstered with luxurious fabrics and others had inset mirrors. The Italians took great pride in commissioning well-known artists to paint their screens. The Victorian ladies, noted for their passion for hand stitching and elaborate decoration, embellished screens with ribbons, pictures, paintings, embroideries, shells and all manner of artifacts.

Today, the screen is a great asset, serving as it does to disguise the ubiquitous television set.

MAKING UP

You will need to have a traditional wooden frame or flat boards. Strip all the fabric from an old screen and cover the surface between the frame with brown paper. Remove any hinges and work with the panels separately. A staple gun or tacks and a tack hammer will be needed to attach the fabric to the wooden frame.

1. Work with one panel at a time. Cut pieces of fabric for both sides of each panel, allowing the fabric to cover the depth of the frame. Start from one side and hold the fabric so that the side edge exactly lines up with the side edge of the wood panel. Staple or tack all the way down, holding the fabric taut but not over-stretching it.

Turn to the opposite side and, making sure that the horizontal line stays true, pull the fabric taut across the panel and fix. Trim away any excess fabric.

2. Staple or tack the top in place, snipping around any shaping. Finish with the base, pulling out any wrinkles. Attach fabric to the back of this panel, overlapping slightly along the side edges but never on to the front or back. Cover all panels in the same way.

3. Cut strips of fabric the length of the screen and at least four times the depths of the side – the fabric hinges which will hold the panels together will need to be wide enough to stretch over two panels when the screen is folded flat. Staple these to two adjacent panels, keeping the raw edges just inside the edge of the panels and ensuring that the staples go right through all layers.

4. Glue or tack braid around each side to hide all raw edges. Fit brass studs to the base of each panel.

Left: To take advantage of a screen, you can use one or both sides as a type of pinboard – to hold photos and mementoes, or for notes and swatches of your colour schemes. Stretch braid across each panel and staple into the sides to hold securely.

Right: A small printed pattern allows the screen to blend in with the surrounding furnishings.

Below: Slipcovers might be the best solution if you have a valuable antique textile on your screen whiach you wish to preserve, for a screen which needs to be moved into another room for a short time, or when a seasonal change is desirable. Left loose at the bottom for easy fitting, the piped outer edge gives some definition and the bows pinned through hold the sections in place.

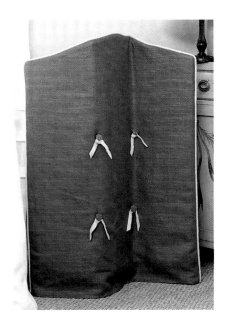

STORAGE

Boxes keep shoes, hats, photos, papers, old school books, maps, games, toys, out-of-season clothes, plus a multitude of other family paraphernalia in check. Select fabrics which don't easily show dirty marks; and vacuum and dust periodically to keep clean.

Storage – or the lack of it – must be one of the biggest headaches for us all, whether at the office or in the home. Shoes, dresses, gloves, toys, greetings cards, photographs, cassettes, bags, maps, magazine cuttings, toiletries, stationery, CD discs and a myriad other things all need homes, and cupboard space is always at a premium. Freestanding cupboards and shelves are only part of the solution – small items still need to be kept together and yet separate from everything else to prevent complete chaos.

Covering boxes with paper or fabric provides an harmonious display which is aesthetically pleasing and will solve many storage problems. Use fabric to make covers for shelves and transform baskets and wooden boxes with fabric covers and lids – they will help keep loose items under control.

Save shoe boxes, hat boxes, chocolate and stationery boxes, aiming to make sets – which are more attractive than many single boxes and easier to plan into open shelving. Even larger boxes – those purchased with small electrical goods or sports equipment, boxes sent with deliveries and others begged from shops – will be useful for storing large clothing items, Christmas decorations, out-of-season wear and essential documents.

The more ambitious can make their own boxes: search the craft magazines for addresses of kit and card suppliers.

SHOE BOXES

Choose sturdy boxes and try to obtain ones of similar size so that they stack up neatly. Or open up one box and lid, and cut the same shapes from 2 mm (⅛ in) cardboard. Score the four sides of each and fold up, tape the ends together, so making a good solid box which can be copied easily. If you want to be able to see into the box without taking the lid off, cut a hole in one end and cover with clear acetate.

MAKING UP

You will need a 2.5 cm (1 in) brush, PVA glue and a suitable working surface.

The Lid

1. Cut a piece of fabric the length and width of the lid, twice the depth of the side, plus 1 cm (½ in). So a lid measuring 30 x 20 cm with a 2.5 cm side will need fabric 30 + 5 + 1 x 20 + 5 + 1, in other words 36 x 26 cm (12 x 8 x 1 in lid: 12 + 2 + ½ x 8 + 2 + ½ = 14½ x 10½ in). Paste a thin layer of glue all over the lid and place centrally on to the fabric. Smooth

thoroughly with the palm of your hand. Glue each long side and pull the fabric over the side of the lid, smoothing the fabric flat. Fold one short end over and pinch the sides together at one corner. Snip away excess fabric, 1 cm (½ in) from the corner. Repeat with the other corner on the same end.

2. Paste the short side of the lid and press down the flaps from the long sides. Paste lightly over these flaps, fold the other flaps under and press the whole side down. Repeat with the other end.

3. Paste inside the long sides of the lid and 1 cm (½ in) on to the inside of the lid. Press the long sides inside, pulling the fabric taut into the crease. Paste the short ends and press the fabric down. To line the lid, take the internal measurements and cut fabric to fit.

The box

4. Cut a piece of fabric the length and width of the box plus 2 cm (¾ in) and the depth of the box plus 3 cm (1¼ in). Paste the four sides with a thin, even layer of glue. Keep the fabric straight with equal overlaps at the top and bottom, starting 1 cm (½ in) on one short side. Follow on to the adjacent long side and then on to the remaining sides, keeping the fabric straight and smoothing out any air bubbles as you go. At the corner, cut the fabric to meet the edge and paste in place.

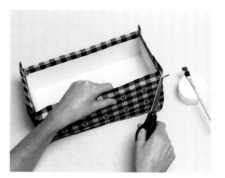

5. Snip down in to each corner and take a tiny nick out. The hole left should be approximately 2 mm (⅛ in) wide. Paste the inside of the box and press each side down in turn, pressing well into the corners and keeping the top edge even.

6. Take the same small strips of fabric from each bottom corner and press under one side at a time, cutting mitres at each end of the long sides to prevent a fabric lump at each corner. Cut a piece of lining for the base, 1 cm (½ in) smaller all round than the base measurements; paste in place.

If you wish to line the inside of the box, cut one piece of fabric to fit all around the four sides and deep enough to start 1 cm (½ in) from the top edge and to paste 1 cm (½ in) on to the inside base. Cut the base piece to fit exactly and paste all over the raw edges.

You might like to pad the top of the box, in which case cut a piece of polyester wadding to the exact size of the box lid and glue in place before covering with fabric. Don't paste the padding, just apply adhesive along the four sides.

Once you discover the satisfaction of making storage boxes you will probably be making and covering them over a period of years – so select fabrics which complement each other in colour and style that will easily mix and match.

HAT BOX

Hat boxes not only make attractive storage for your own use, but are also marvellous gifts for special friends. The type of box supplied with a hat is perfect to cover, but as not all hats are supplied with boxes, you can also buy papier mâché or strong cardboard ones from most craft shops and mail order suppliers.

MAKING UP

You will need a glue brush approximately 2.5 cm (1 in) wide, PVA glue, brown paper and a suitable working surface.

The lid

1. Cut one piece of fabric to fit the top plus 1.5 cm (⅝ in) all around. Cut another piece to measure the circumference of the box plus 2 cm (¾ in) and three times the depth of the lid plus 3 cm (1¼ in).

Hat boxes are essential to protect any hat from dust or strong sunlight, whether the indispensable winter trilby or the summer wedding extravagance, but they can also be used for a much wider array of other things, like scarves, belts and toiletries.

2. To cover the lid, spread a thin layer of glue evenly all over the card and place the fabric centrally on top. Smooth out any air bubbles with your hand. Snip into the excess fabric all around almost up to the card. Paste around the side of the lid and carefully press the snipped edge down, holding until each section is secure and making sure to keep the top edge even and the fabric pulled taut.

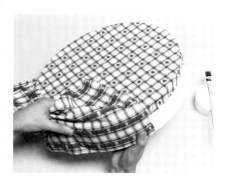

3. Paste the side of the lid and press the other piece of fabric around as shown, keeping the raw edge just 1 mm (¹⁄₁₆ in) above the bottom edge of the card. Overlap the join neatly and leave to dry.

4. Taking care to keep the top edge of the fabric level with the top of the lid, fold the fabric back down. Paste inside the sides and just 1.5 cm (⅝ in) on to the inner lid. Press the fabric strip inside and into place. Run a needle around the crease to keep the fabric flat.

To line the inside of the lid, take the inner diameter measurement and cut one piece of fabric to fit exactly. Paste and press in place.

The base

5. Cut a length of fabric the circumference of the box plus 2 cm (¾ in) and the depth of the box plus 7 cm (2¾ in). Paste the box side and place the fabric on top with 5 cm (2 in) spare above and 2 cm (¾ in) below. Smooth out and overlap neatly at the join. Glue one brush width around the base. Snip the bottom 2 cm (¾ in) of fabric and press on to the base. Cut fabric to cover the base, just 1 cm (⅜ in) smaller than the box base. Glue the 5 cm (2 in) spare at the top to the inside. Glue ribbon over the raw edge, finishing with a neat bow.

If you prefer to line the inside of the box, glue a length of fabric around the inside, and 1 cm (⅜ in) on to the base. Cover with a circle of fabric the exact dimensions of the inside base.

BASKETS

PICNIC BASKET

Picnicking by a river or in the woods is the ultimate summer pleasure for many travellers and day trippers. A well equipped and attractive picnic basket was probably one of our best investments and the only practical way to feed and water three small children as we travelled. So our picnic basket and rugs are always in the back of the car, although as we have grown older, there are now also fold-up chairs and padded covers.

Fabric basket linings are not only highly decorative but also extremely practical – plates, glasses and food can be kept safely in as many sections as you wish to make. Another bonus is that these linings are the only way I have found to prevent sand and dirt creeping through the wicker base and sides.

MAKING UP

1. Measure all around the inside of the basket and the depth. Add 1.5 cm (⅝ in) for seam allowances and 5 per cent for quilting shrinkage. Cut out two pieces. Measure the base, add the same allowances and cut two pieces.

2. Place one side piece on the worktable, right side down, and tack 150 g (6 oz) polyester wadding all around. Place the opposite piece over, right side up. Pin and tack together all around, and through all layers at 10 cm (4 in) intervals. Checked fabrics have good natural grid lines for you to follow. Mark out your quilting design with pins and then with a light pencil and large tacks. To prevent the fabrics moving while stitching, pin regularly at right angles over each line.

3. Quilt through all layers. Decide at this stage how many pockets you want, cut them out and place them along the sides, pinning securely. Slip the lining back into the basket and check that the items you want to use will slide in and out of the pockets easily. Stitch the pockets in place and join the side seam.

4. Quilt the base in the same way and stitch to the sides. Bind the raw edges with self fabric strips.

5. Make pairs of ties either from the same fabric or using coloured tapes, each at least 20 cm (8 in) in length. Pin to the inside of the top raw edge. Bind the top with coloured binding, press the ties to the top and top stitch to reinforce. Press, slip the lined pad into the basket base and tie on.

DESIGN AND MAKE DECORATIVE DETAILS

6. Make a similar pad for the basket lid, cutting out, pinning and quilting as before. Cut 20 cm (8 in) lengths, hem one on the raw edge, and pin along both short sides. Stitch around the three outer edges, and stitch through at regular intervals to make cutlery pockets, checking that your cutlery will slide in and out easily, but tightly enough to prevent it falling out. Position your ties and stitch binding all around to enclose the raw edges. Tie in place.

STORAGE BASKETS

Baskets provide attractive storage especially when fitted with a fabric to conceal the contents within. To make a fabric basket lid, measure the diameter or length and breadth of your basket opening. Cut two pieces of fabric, one for the top and one for the lining. To these measurements add 2 cm (¾ in) in each direction for 'shrinkage' and 1.5 cm (⅝ in) all around for seams. Make up a frill to fit all around and insert between the top and bottom pieces. Fill with a piece of foam approximately 2 cm (¾ in) deep, or two layers of wadding. Make fastenings to suit your basket – employing ties, buttons, eyelets, laces and ribbons, as appropriate.

Other baskets which might benefit from a lid or a lid and lining might hold bread for the table, bathroom toiletries, cosmetics, hairbands and bracelets on a dressing table, pens and pencils on a kitchen dresser, CDs and cassettes or laundry, to mention just a few.

Top: An attractive rustic basket is a good home for occasional toys which are kept neat and tidy with pretty fabric lids. The eyelet and shoelace fastenings are easy to make, to undo for laundering and allow the lid to slide easily on and off.

Bottom: For those magazines with which you are loathe to part, but concerned to store, make a decorative frill. Allow approximately one-and-a-half times fullness for basket linings or decorative frills. Long ties wind around the handles looping into bows.

SHOE BAGS

These marvellous devices are designed to hold shoes in the suitcase – also the hairdryer, books, cosmetics, lingerie and to bring home the dirty washing. Because they can be made in any size, the number of possible uses for these bags seems to grow daily, especially as they are handy around the house for washing, linen, and anything else you want to store.

To make this simple bag, fold a length of fabric in half with the right side inside and stitch along the two sides. Fold the open edge under twice to conceal the raw edge and stitch close to both fold lines. Leave a small opening near one seam to insert cord or tape which will be pulled up to close the opening. Or fit eyelets through all layers and thread through with thick cotton cord. If you want to make a contrast lining, make up two bags the same size and insert the inner into the outer before making the cord casing.

CLOTHES COVERS

Long and short clothes bags hold suits, jackets and dresses in storage between seasons, or protect clothing while travelling. These really don't take long to make and once you have cut out the first one, all the others will be the same – just adjust the length as necessary. If you already own a suit cover, use it as a template to make your own; if not, base the top shaping around the size of a suit hanger and add approximately 7 cm (2¾ in) extra to the width at each side.

For a single item, the front and back of the bag could just be stitched together, but if you want to store several items in one bag, a gusset – cut to whatever depth you need – all around will allow the bag to expand. Similarly, the hole at the top can be cut large enough to take several hangers or small enough for one. The flap on the front of the cover shown here opens so that the clothes can be dropped inside – no dust can creep in – but a vertical front opening, buttoned or tied to close, would be a satisfactory alternative.

As with shoe bags, clothes bags need to be made from fabric which is easy to launder and press, in colours which will harmonize with your bedroom or dressing room. Washed denim chambray is a good universal choice as it can be masculine or feminine, and will team up well with strong checks or pretty floral prints.

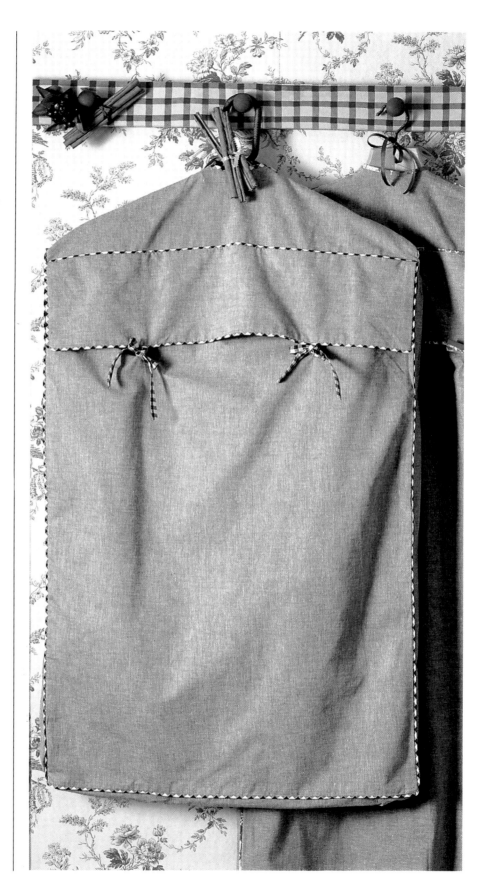

COVERING SHELVES

Do-it-yourself kits or ready-made shelving units can be bought inexpensively in almost any size and finish, to fit into small corners or over whole walls. Covering the shelves with fabric or paper covering, whether you choose to cover just the sides or the whole, will improve and personalise these units. While adding a curtain to the front extends the use of otherwise decorative shelving, transforming it into a complete storage area.

Curtains can be fitted to lift up, draw to one side, zip together in the centre, or to pull up as blinds, depending on the style of shelving and your chosen usage. While almost any fabric could be used, cottons need not cost the earth and are easy to work with. You will need to be able to pull the fabric taut without it stretching unnecessarily, be able to finger press folds and it must be possible to cut in a straight line without a problem. An all-over print is most forgiving, hiding almost any mistakes; stripes look smart but have to be matched and kept vertical, checks look very good but can be problematical – matching up in both directions is never straightforward.

A staple gun is useful for holding the fabric at the back of the shelves, but glue will be needed to hold the fabric to the front and tops of shelves. A water soluble glue which adheres fairly quickly but doesn't mark fabric is essential. Check a small piece of fabric first to make sure that the glue does not seep through too readily.

Simple designs could be painted or stencilled to a plain heavy fabric, such as denim. Try balloons, cars, teddies, trains or animals for a child's bedroom or toy storage, and perhaps fishing or golfing symbols for dedicated storage. Wide stripes are evocative of circus tents, fun for small children, and could be decorated with circus animals and clowns. Tent canvas is probably too heavy-duty to use for covering shelves but is perfect for an overall tented covering held together with cords threaded through eyelets. Towelling could be used for a bathroom, floral cotton chintz for a dressing room, a simple gingham check to hold the saucepans.

Above: This simple fabric, strongly woven with a crisp stripe, resembles old-fashioned mattress ticking. It makes these shelves smart enough to suit almost any situation.

Below: The shelves of antique glass cupboards were almost never left bare. Covering with fabric is a traditional alternative to painting. Choose fabric in keeping with the style and quality of your furniture, so select silk for a Georgian corner machine or a small country print for a pine linen chest.

MAKING UP

For shelves such as those shown on the right, you will need to use newspaper to make templates before cutting them, as it is extremely rare to find two walls which meet at perfect right angles. Neat battens screwed to the wall hold the shelves in place.

The shelves inside linen presses and wardrobes can be covered with fabric instead of the usual paper sheets. Sprinkle your favourite eau de cologne on to the fabric to keep the linen smelling fresh. Often the edges of shelves were decorated with strips of lace or paper cut outs, but any ribbon or braid in the right colour and style will look attractive.

To cover a unit with fixed shelves, start with the two sides. Cut two lengths longer than the shelving unit and wide enough to cover from the back around the inside to return to the back.

Holding the fabric vertically, staple it to the back of the side along the length of the unit. Bring the fabric to the front and glue to the narrow front piece, keeping any stripes and checks in line. To accommodate each shelf, take one at a time, snip along the width to line up with the centre of the shelf and snip back so that a V shape is left at the front of the shelf. Glue this piece in place. Taking the fabric above the shelf, bring it around to the back. Paste the flap on to the top of the shelf and staple the back piece over the first edge. Repeat with each shelf.

To cover the shelves, cut fabric the width of the shelf plus 3 cm (1¼ in) and long enough to wrap

right around. Press the side raw edges under so that the remaining piece fits exactly the inside width of the shelf. Staple to the outside back of the shelf, keeping the raw edge and the shelf edge lined up. Bring the fabric over the shelf, covering the glued down side flaps and the V shapes on the front. Pull taut and staple at the back to overlap the first edge.

Cover the top in the same way and secure the base to suit the unit construction.

Sometimes there will be a raw edge which is impossible to hide, or you may have an error on the front edges. Don't worry. Cover with a petersham ribbon and nail in place with upholstery pins.

Above: Wood offcuts were made to fit the corner space and covered with a lovely provençal print. Strips of fabric are pinned casually to create an attractive edge at the front of each one.

Below: A neat solution when covering the front of a shelf unit. Brass eyelets pressed through the curtain drop over metal cup hooks which have been screwed into the top of the bookcase.

INDEX